MW01250920

The Earth's Prevailing Wind Belts

By Myrl Shireman
Illustrated By John E. Kaufmann

COPYRIGHT © 2006 Mark Twain Media, Inc.

ISBN 1-58037-370-4

Printing No. D04125

Mark Twain Media, Inc., Publishers
Distributed by Carson-Dellosa Publishing Company, Inc.

Level 5: Book 3

No matter where you are on Earth, you are likely to live in one of the earth's major wind belts. In each of these wind belts, the winds on most days blow from the same direction.

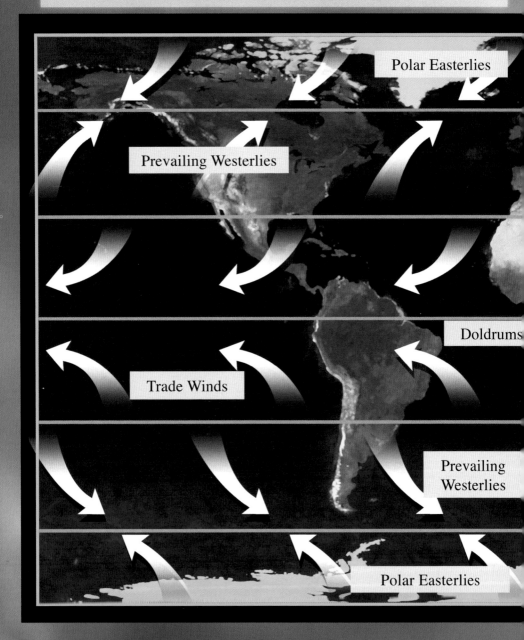

Polar Easterlies

Prevailing Westerlies

Doldrums

Trade Winds

Prevailing Westerlies

Polar Easterlies

Such winds are called **prevailing winds**. These winds bring days of stormy weather and days of sunny weather. Some days, the winds are very calm. On other days, the winds blow very hard.

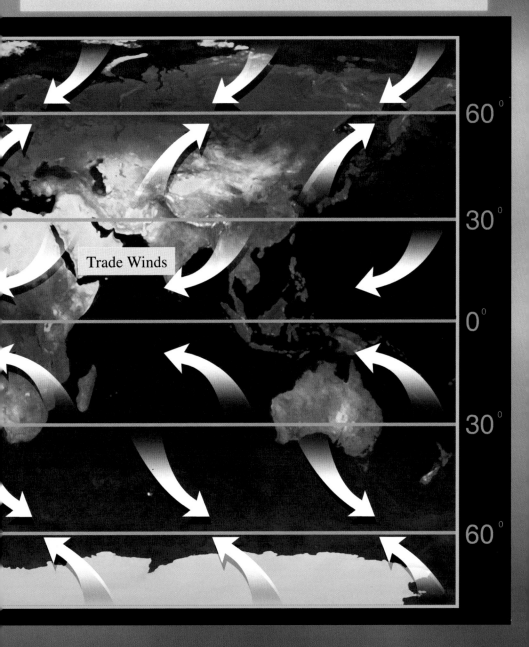

Trade Winds

60°

30°

0°

30°

60°

Major Wind Belts

There are three major wind belts north and south of the equator. The winds in each wind belt do not blow directly north and south. The earth has a spherical shape and rotates on its axis. Because the earth is a sphere, it rotates fastest at the equator. This difference in rotating speed causes the wind belts to be deflected.

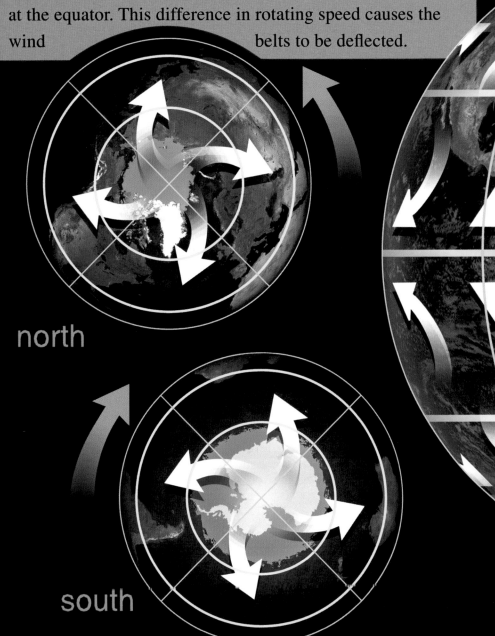

north

south

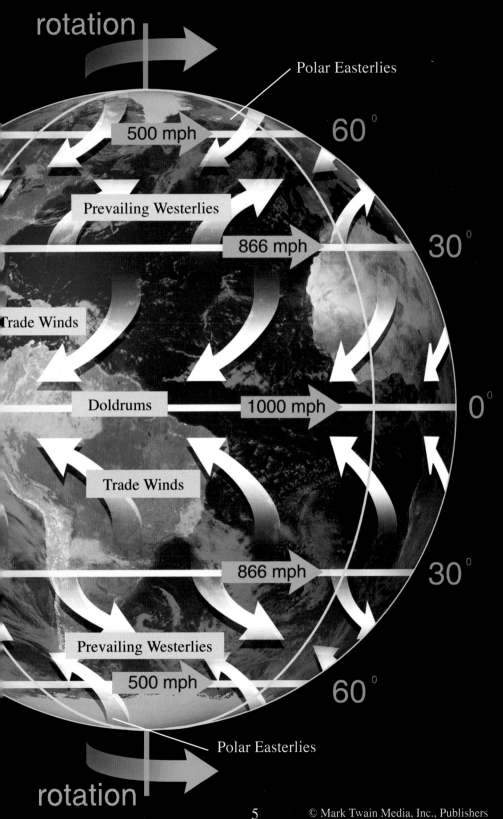

rotation

Polar Easterlies

60°

500 mph

Prevailing Westerlies

866 mph

30°

Trade Winds

Doldrums — 1000 mph

0°

Trade Winds

866 mph

30°

Prevailing Westerlies

500 mph

60°

Polar Easterlies

rotation

5   © Mark Twain Media, Inc., Publishers

Trade Wind Belts

The trade wind belts are located between the equator and 30 degrees north and south latitude. The **northeast trade winds** blow from the northeast toward the southwest. The **southeast trade winds** blow from the southeast toward the northwest. Storms that form over the warm ocean waters are carried west by the trade winds.

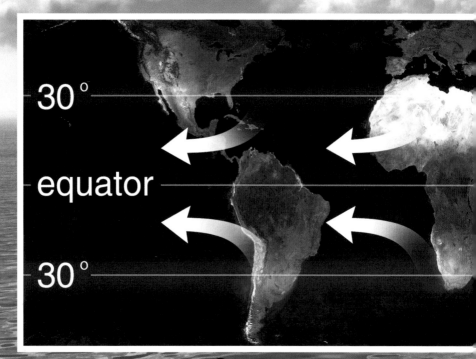

30°

equator

30°

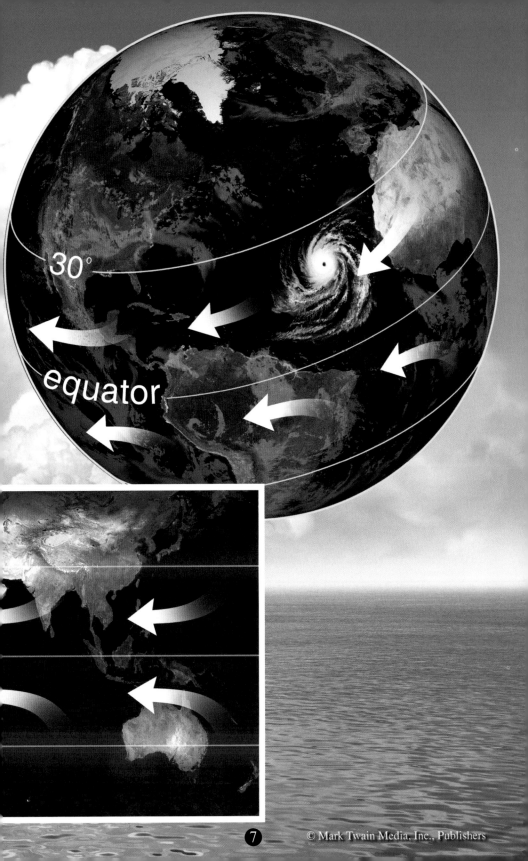

30°

equator

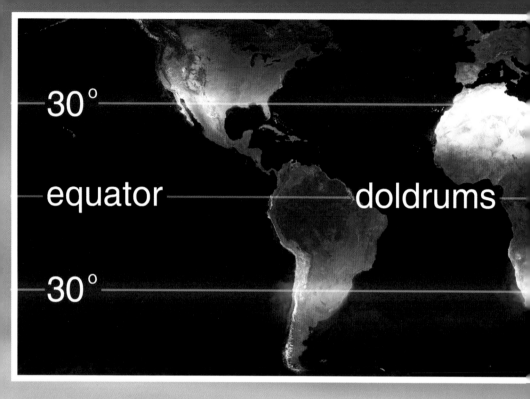

30°

equator   doldrums

30°

Doldrums

Near the equator, there is a region known as the **doldrums**. The doldrums are not a wind belt. In the doldrums, the air is settling down to the earth's surface. Therefore, on most days in the doldrums, there is very little wind. The winds that blow in the doldrums are very inconsistent. The winds may blow from the north, south, east, or west. Often for long periods of time, there is little, if any, wind.

In the days of sailing ships, captains tried to steer clear of the doldrums. Captains knew that a sailing ship in the doldrums might not move for days.

doldrums

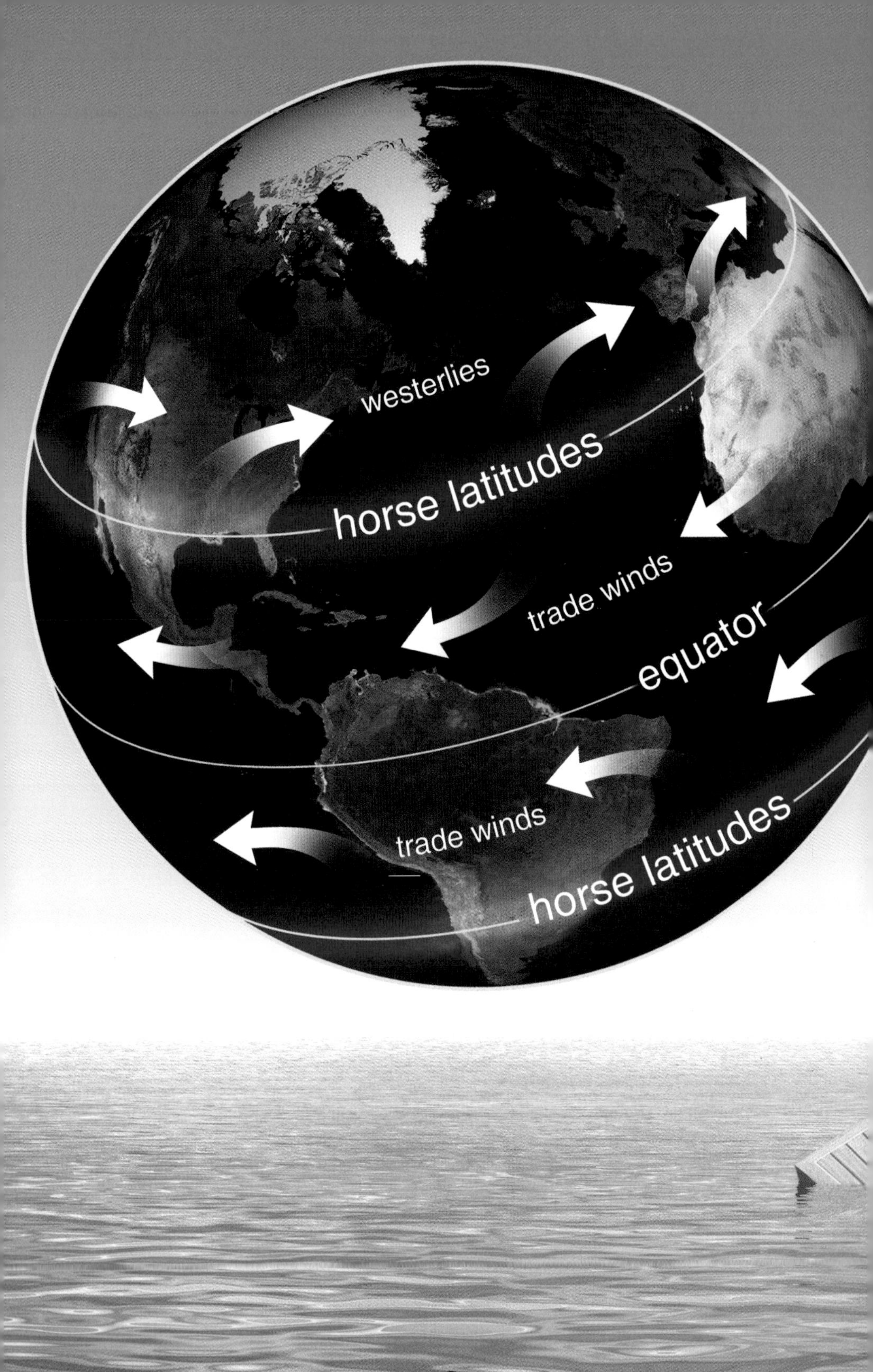

westerlies

horse latitudes

trade winds

equator

trade winds

horse latitudes

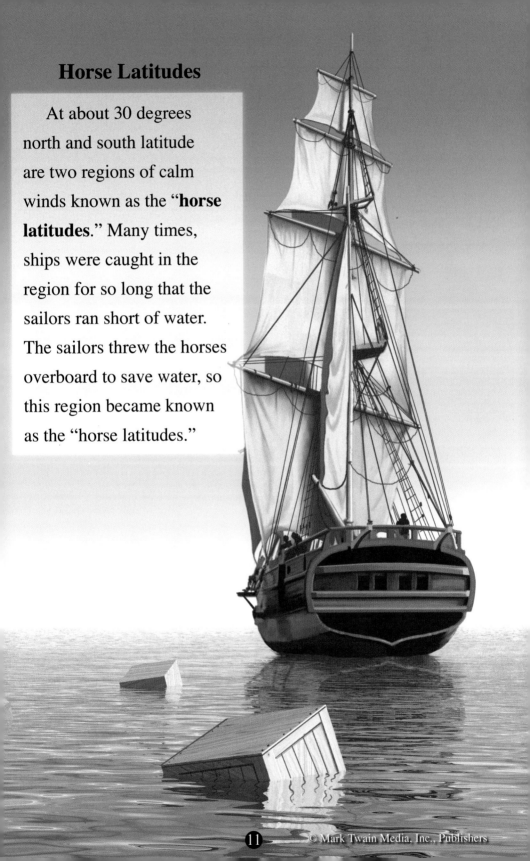

Horse Latitudes

At about 30 degrees north and south latitude are two regions of calm winds known as the "**horse latitudes**." Many times, ships were caught in the region for so long that the sailors ran short of water. The sailors threw the horses overboard to save water, so this region became known as the "horse latitudes."

Westerly Wind Belts

The **westerly wind belts** are located between 30 and 60 degrees north and south latitude. North of the equator, these winds blow from the southwest toward the northeast. South of the equator, the winds blow from the northwest toward the southeast. North or south, the storms that form usually approach from the west and are guided eastward in this wind belt. When the storm passes, the winds will again blow from the southwest or the northwest.

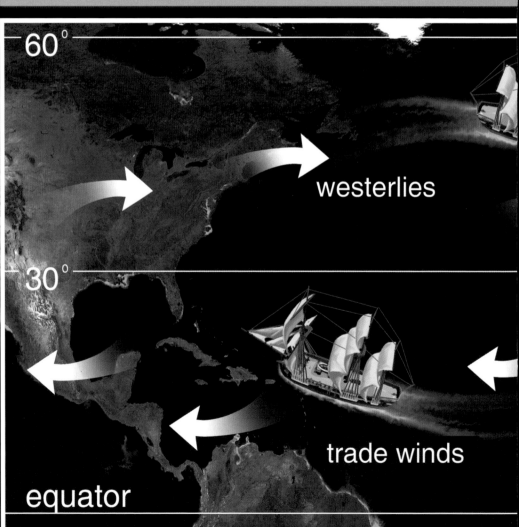

60°

westerlies

30°

trade winds

equator

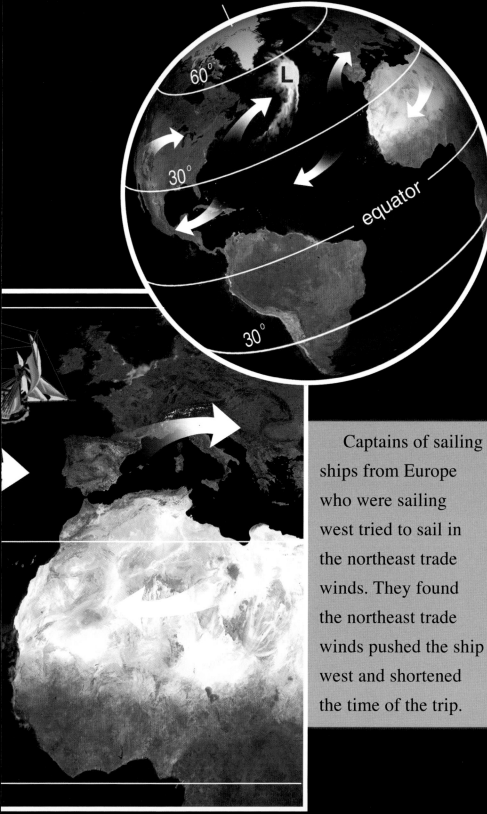

Captains of sailing ships from Europe who were sailing west tried to sail in the northeast trade winds. They found the northeast trade winds pushed the ship west and shortened the time of the trip.

13

However, on the return trip to Europe, the sea captains did not want to sail in the northeast trade winds. Sailing east, they would have to sail against the trade winds. So on the return trip, the ships sailed with the westerly wind belt, and the west winds pushed the ships toward Europe.

Polar Easterlies

The **polar easterlies** are wind belts in which the winds blow from the North Pole toward the southwest and

30°

30°

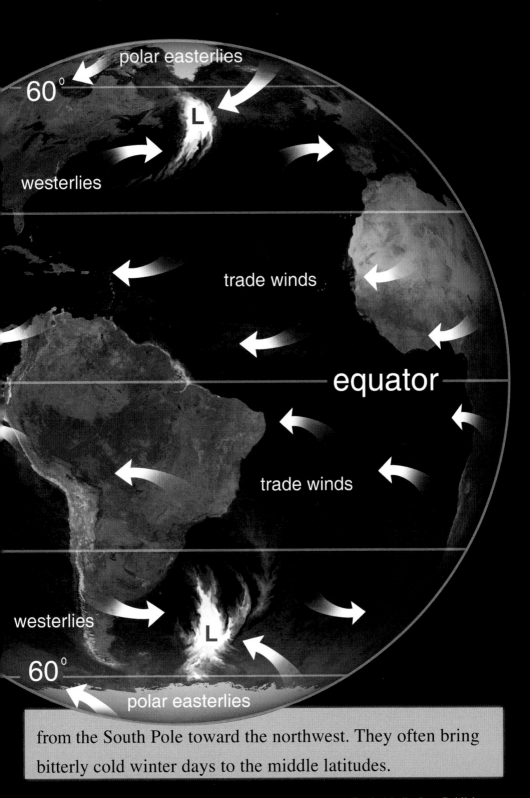

polar easterlies

60°

L

westerlies

trade winds

equator

trade winds

westerlies

L

60°

polar easterlies

from the South Pole toward the northwest. They often bring
bitterly cold winter days to the middle latitudes.

Along the front where these cold winds meet the warmer westerlies, severe winter storms often develop. These winter storms bring ice and snow to many parts of the world. The earth's prevailing winds affect us daily here on Earth.